MY CAT LIKES MILK

By Nancy Prasad

Illustrated by Margaret Power

HOUGHTON MIFFLIN COMPANY

BOSTON

ATLANTA   DALLAS   GENEVA, ILLINOIS   PALO ALTO   PRINCETON

My cat likes milk
and so do I.

2

My cat likes eggs
and so do I.

My cat likes porridge
and so do I.

4

We always eat breakfast together.

My cat eats cheese
and asks for more.

6

My cat eats bacon
and licks his whiskers.

He eats ice cream
and purrs louder.

We always eat lunch together.

But, my cat likes fish
that isn't cooked.

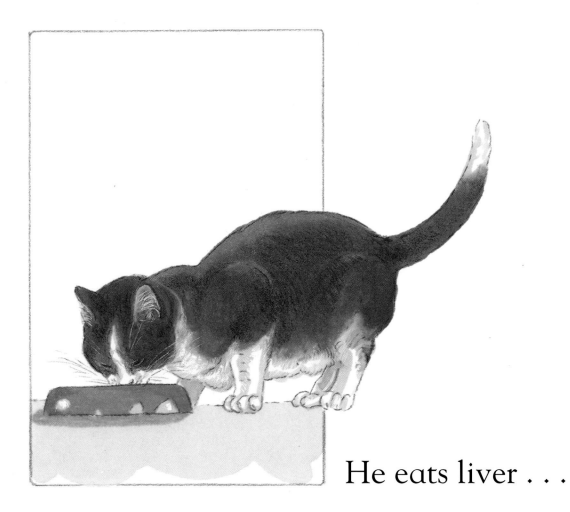

He eats liver . . .

and kidney and heart.

He hunts frogs . . .

We separate for supper.